Hitting the Sweet Spot

HITTING THE SWEET SPOT

DISCOVER
HOW TO BE MORE
AUTHENTIC,
ADMIRABLE, AND AMAZING
IN
HOSPITALITY INDUSTRY

Evelyn Waterhouse

The Amazing Company

St. Catharines, Ontario

Evelyn Waterhouse/The Amazing Company
17 Tremont Drive
St. Catharines, Ontario L2A 3A7
http://www.iamamazing.ca

Ordering Information:
Quantity sales. Special discounts are available on quantity purchases by corporations, associations, and others. For details, contact the "Special Sales Department" at the address above.

Hitting the Sweet Spot/ Evelyn Waterhouse. —1st ed.
ISBN 978-0-9939094-1-2

For

Joseph, Paolina,

Christopher, and Catherine

Table of Content

"Acknowledgement and celebration are essential to fueling passion making people feel valid and valuable, and giving the team a real sense of progress that makes it all worthwhile."

—Dwight Frindt

I WOULD LIKE TO TAKE THIS opportunity to express a heart feel thank you to a few people.

A few years ago, while working at a large buffet in a gaming facility, a gentleman waited for me at the front of the restaurant. A co-worker had informed me that he wanted to speak to me directly. How intriguing! As I approached, I could tell that this gentleman was not a gamer: working in the industry for as long as I had, you can tell who a gamer is and who is not.

I approached and asked him if there was anything I could do for him. He informed me that he had been observing me while I was working and said that I had a beautiful smile. Of course, I flashed that smile and said playfully, "Great, I have a stalker!"

We giggled for a moment and he asked me, "Why do you smile so much when you're working?"

"Because I love it," I responded. "The smile is in the eyes, not on the lips. Always look for the smile in the eyes, it will show that you are in love."

"You should write a book about what you do," the gentleman suggested.

"Would you read it?" I inquired.

"Yes, I would and so would others," he said.

Taken aback, I responded, "I do what I do because I love it. I wouldn't know how to begin to write a book about it. I do thank you for taking the time. How nice it was to have met you. I wish you an amazing evening."

And we parted ways without me asking his name. So, to you, my mystery gentleman, I thank you for planting a seed of inspiration to write a book about what I love.

I would also like to give my appreciation and acknowledgment to Executive Chef Raymond Taylor. Chef Taylor supported me while I worked at the buffet and was the first person to ever request my thoughts or ideas in any workplace. This was a totally new experience, and my first time being thus acknowledged by a person in a leadership role. I thank you, Chef, for taking the time to listen to my ideas, and to implement my recommendations, all the while establishing a positive, harmless banter-filled workplace in which open communication, creativity, and innovation were sought after. Thank you for your support and your encouragement in my passion as a host, and for your leadership qualities. I am so fortunate to have worked with someone who accepted me and recognized my passion, humour, and humility, and who always encouraged me to believe that I *can* rather than that I *can't*. I thank you for embracing my silliness and my seriousness with an understanding that in life, we need to strive to find balance both at home and in the workplace. Thank you for teaching me the importance of this balance, and of walking the fine line between giving and receiving—especially when times are tough. Because of you, I have learned that these efforts will foster a harmonious workplace in which growth and sustainability are achievable.

To Skylar, my editor. Words are not enough to express my gratitude. I wish you all the best in your studies towards obtaining your PhD in English.

"The best conversations are the ones where you don't have to worry about what you say, you can just be you."

—*Unknown*

H I, HOW YOU DOING? ME, I'M AMAZING—thank you very much.

I want to share with you the story of how the title of this book, **Hitting the Sweet Spot**, came about. Let me tell you, I must have changed the title three times before I finally settled on **Hitting the Sweet Spot**. For those of you that play any sport using a bat, club, racket, or paddle, you've heard this expression before: the **Sweet Spot** is the part of your equipment that will generate the greatest amount of velocity and the greatest results possible. It is the most effective contact point for knocking the ball out of the park—and who doesn't want to do that?! Achieving this consistently is not as easy as sports professionals make it look, though. Top performers know how to **Hit the Sweet Spot**, but they also understand that they are only as good as their last game. To improve their abilities and to advance to the next level requires more than just an awareness of where to find the **Sweet Spot**: a positive attitude is needed, too—though maybe not for someone like John McEnroe! Added to this positive attitude is a deep sense of care, an ability to focus, and a willingness to take responsibility for improving their game.

What I realized while thinking about these values and practices is that they are totally applicable beyond a sports arena. I came to this book's title when I realized that the practices needed to **Hit the Sweet Spot** were exactly those that were needed to succeed in the business environments in which I had worked. I think that achieving the greatest possible results should be the goal or the end game of the work day. So, let's step it up a notch. Let's see how we can improve our performance, communicate better, be better human beings, and become better "players" than we are today—all while having fun, uplifting one another, and sharing positivity with our colleagues. There has never been a sports figure or prominent social leader that didn't have to practice and be willing to let go of their perceived failures to become better than they were the day before. So, with that in mind, I encourage you to read this book with an open mind, and to understand that finding the **Sweet Spot** will take courage, vulnerability and a willingness to recognize that *you* can shift your attitude towards improving your work in the Hospitality Industry by critically reflecting on your habits, values, and goals. As you read **Hitting the Sweet Spot**, you'll notice that, taking my own advice, I have left myself vulnerable by sharing personal stories selected to serve as case studies which illustrate the importance of the lessons outlined in the following pages. Only with bravery, patience and humility have I been able to come to these conclusions. I hope you can do the same—and that this book helps you along the way.

Enjoy.

"Spend more time smiling than frowning and more time praising than criticizing."

—Richard Branson

ARE YOU SOMEONE WHO HAS BEEN lucky enough to discover their *thing* in life? How did you know when you found it—was it a "eureka!" moment? If a hobby, passion, or interest of yours immediately sprang to mind when you read these questions, take a second to consider this: how would you go about describing what it is you love and why you're drawn to it? Do you think you could convince someone from another galaxy, totally unfamiliar with the ways of our world, to be inspired by your passion and energy for your *thing*?

Sometimes it's as easy as just saying that you love whatever your *thing* may be—cars, music, math, cooking, nature, and so on. The list could go on forever! On that note, though, there's a big difference between stating your passion in a straightforward way and planting a seed of inspiration and purpose in others. I'm a lucky person, as far as finding my *thing* goes—but we'll get back to my story soon enough. For now, I want you to think about this book as a project in passion—both my own, and the passion I'd like to encourage others to develop.

Before I ever found the words to articulate what it means to **Hit the Sweet Spot,** I had to ask myself a few questions. First and foremost: how can I frame my thinking about something that I love, something that comes naturally to me, to understanding it as something that can be dissected, described, and taught? Is it really possible to make others feel the way I feel? Seeing someone in their element or doing the *thing* they love might make this process look easy, but it's not. It's a beautiful experience, watching people do their *thing*: can we turn the recognition of that beauty into a desire to learn about what others love, or to see passion as a transmittable feeling?

In this book, I'm going to try to talk about my *thing* in a way that hopefully inspires you to become more passionate about your own experiences in frontline service. Through the self-reflection methods I describe in **Hitting the Sweet Spot**, I realized that I can take what I love, get excited about it, and embrace it—in a way that will encourage others to be excited about it, too.

I was watching a video the other day about a well-known actress. At age 70, she had not retired, but had found the freedom while working to be able to do what she loves—her *thing*—outside of her employment, which itself undoubtedly requires a strong sense of devotion.

Her face lit up when she spoke about her *thing*, and her sense of passion for it radiated from the inside out. But what was the source of this joy?

For her, it was all about trees! With the financial freedom she had procured from her work, this actress was able to purchase a large piece of green, flourishing, tree-filled land. Her love for trees inspired her to learn about them, their growth, and their importance, and her learning inspired her to share her knowledge to help the world discover their significance. By purchasing the land for herself, this actress had found a way to embrace what she loves on her own terms. More important than that, though, she chose to allow other people the opportunity to hear her message, share in her passion, and come to her and say, "you know what, I feel the same thing as you do. We can all come together to think about the world's well-being." Isn't that beautiful? Talk about **Hitting the Sweet Spot!**

The feeling is like none other, but I can compare it to the pleasure of watching a perfectly choreographed dance. There's something magical about seeing dancers move their bodies in a way that looks effortless as they cross the dancefloor. But I know that looking effortless isn't always the whole story. Those graceful, elegant dancers had to start somewhere. Their passion for dance involved a learning process, too. Talent and innate ability can't be overlooked, but to develop the skills that dancers have can involve years and years of practice. In a way, **Hitting the Sweet Spot** is about building on the capabilities that so many frontline associates already possess, and transforming the feeling of working with short-term obligation into one that inspires long-term intention and purpose.

Everybody has to start somewhere: when it came time to write this book, I knew that I had to look deep inside of myself to figure out how my "dance" might look effortless to others. For me, it's all about the Hospitality

Industry. While it seems a far cry from trees, I promise that I'm quite like the actress I told you about a few pages ago: I shine brightest when I'm doing my *thing*. You can hear it in my voice and see it in my eyes: I have totally embraced Hospitality and want nothing more than to inspire others to try to do the same.

I had to ask myself what skills and techniques I've learned along the way to the **Sweet Spot**. I also had to get in touch with how and when these processes began to come more naturally to me, and with how the challenges I have faced along the way helped to shape the person I've become. More than anything else, I knew that it was about figuring out the building blocks that helped me to get to where I am today. In this book, I'm going to share those steps with you. Just like our tree-loving actress, my passions have also inspired me to try to share the knowledge and skills that I've acquired to try to make the world a better place—and that starts with you!

"From the moment I wake up, to the moment I go to bed, everyone I meet is my customer."

—*Evelyn Waterhouse*

DURING MY FAVOURITE YEARS working in the Hospitality Industry, I was employed as a hostess in a 650-seat buffet-style restaurant housed in one of Niagara Falls' casinos. I had worked in the casino as a cashier, seamstress and server prior to becoming a hostess, but it wasn't until taking on this role that I fell head-over-heels in love with my work. The position was one thing, and I enjoyed the job itself; the venue, though, was another matter entirely. Every time I went to work, I was lucky enough to take in a stunning view of Niagara

Falls. I developed such a strong sense of gratitude for being able to work in that incredible environment that it was hard not to want to give it my all whenever I clocked in.

Thinking back, I can't help but lovingly remember how amazing that feeling was—and how often I got to bask in it. It was enough to give me tingles all over my body. The sensation of being so inspired and comfortable that I felt at home for the first time in a work environment was phenomenal. The views were truly breathtaking, and they blew me away. I knew that this place would be where I wanted to **Hit the Sweet Spot**. But it wasn't always easy. Sometimes, it meant learning how to take the good days and the bad days with a sense of humor and gratitude. More than anything, it's about the sense of fulfilment you can manifest when you rise above the office politics, distractions, and other potential hang-ups in the workplace that could deter you from reaching your goals. This book is full of anecdotes drawn from my years at the buffet: because I felt so strongly about my work, my experiences there helped to form my sense of self. In the next few chapters, I'll refer to my days spent there often— it's hard to resist talking about the thing you love most! Working in the buffet also meant developing an awareness of how each department within the casino works together to ensure that every customer's experience is an amazing one. In this book, I focus on the role of the frontline service associate in strengthening their relationships with both their customers and their administrative, executive, and managerial coworkers.

Hitting the Sweet Spot is about the magic that happens when we engage whole-heartedly with each other towards a common goal. It can be an interesting challenge to identify all the connections and interrelations in your workplace—but have no doubt, in one way or another, social, fiscal, or professional, under the same company, all employees are connected. When you frame your thinking this way, you can see the community that exists in your workplace. When you see yourself as part of this community, you may feel a stronger sense of responsibility to represent it well. I know that I did.

"A strong friendship doesn't need daily conversation or togetherness. As long as the relationship lives in the heart, true friends never part."

—*Unknown*

M EET *THE THREE AMIGOS*. Before I introduce you to these very good friends, it's important to first establish that, while they are very distinct, all three have value and purpose, especially when they work together. *The Three Amigos* are at peak performance when they respect each other for their individual qualities and abilities, and when they appreciate what one can do for the other with these skills. They are aware that no one Amigo is any more important than the other. That is why they are friends. But before we start to look at these friends closely, I want to take a second to describe the world in which they operate.

Not unlike other business sectors, the Hospitality Industry has defining characteristics. One of the most significant of these traits is a major focus on—and interest in—increasing customer satisfaction. Hospitality is a leisure industry that relies on its patrons' disposable income and available leisure time. Above all else, the Hospitality Industry is designed for customers from all walks of life to enjoy and take pleasure in their chosen getaway. Benchmark companies in Hospitality must keep a close eye on local and global economic conditions which can affect the flow of customers: it's not outside of your job description, if you work in the Industry, to stay up to speed with major local and world events in order to create a better, more thoughtful experience for your patrons.

Think of the Hospitality Industry as a wide umbrella, encompassing but not limited to cruise ships, private sporting clubs, hotels, tourism, and even some airlines. I say some airlines because air travel has, in recent years, become a more widely accessible, less leisurely experience: travel is often perceived as a necessary evil along the way to a comfortable end, rather than as the comfort itself— but this isn't always the case, as first-class flyers likely know all too well.

You may wish to spend your disposable income and leisure time at the luxury of the Ritz-Carlton Hotel in Toronto or getting in touch with your inner child by exploring Disney World in Florida. I have done and embraced both! Both examples, the Ritz-Carlton and Disney, are the best of the best in their respective markets. The hotel and the park exceed their customers' expectations. What sustains these two legendary companies—and promises their growth and development in the years to come—is that both are committed to creating a high service standard for the Hospitality Industry, and to striving to deliver results that exceed this standard every time. Another good example of service excellence and the growth it can enable is Richard Branson's Virgin Group, which is now making its mark on the Hospitality Industry with Virgin Hotels. What I have noticed about these companies is that their spirit often comes from the vision of a single person. Walt Disney's passion and soul went into creating the Disney dynasty, for example: he had love in his heart, not green. César Ritz set the bar high for luxury hotels at the end of the nineteenth century, going as far as establishing the César Ritz College in Switzerland, which is focused on hospitality, tourism, business and hotel management. Talk about paying it forward!

There is an important distinction between embracing the vison, passion, and spirit of a person on one hand, and trying to copy, impersonate, or duplicate these qualities on the other. When a corporation tries to build their individual foundation upon another company's vision, something is lost along the way: not only is the heart, soul, and energy of the startup jeopardized, but the original company's intention may be misrepresented or improperly executed. A lot of companies try to follow in the footsteps of the best of the best in the industry, but this effort doesn't always work in such a straightforward way. It's about developing a sense of intention that serves your company's purpose—and tapping into this spirit every day, with every customer. Emulating the qualities of major corporations is a step in the right direction, but only insofar as it serves your company's needs and values. So, where do frontline staff fit into this picture?

Me, I like to think of the answer to this question through music. You'll find as you read through **Hitting the Sweet Spot** that I occasionally use music as a tool to relate my message. Here, it's "Mambo No. 5" by Lou Bega—but we're going to change up the words a bit.

…A little bit of Disney in my life,

A little bit of Virgin by my side,

A little bit of Ritz is all I need…

You get the idea. When you take the most admirable qualities of the most successful players in the Industry and bring them together in your own work—with respect to proportion!—you can create an amazing customer service experience that will exceed customer expectations. **Hitting the Sweet Spot** is about getting in touch with your natural gifts, skills, and capabilities to ensure that your company's values, mission, and purpose are being effectively communicated and achieved. Look to the best of the best for inspiration—but be aware of your limits and your needs as an employee. This is how to provide amazing customer service.

Just like "Mambo No. 5," the Hospitality Industry requires a precisely measured mix of the right people, skills, qualities, and values to succeed. No two companies are alike—but there are qualities shared by many sectors of the Hospitality Industry that can be improved upon through self-reflection and teamwork. The goal of this next section is to introduce these qualities via a learning tool that I've entitled *The Three Amigos*: interconnected yet separate "friends" in the Hospitality Industry who *already* work together to get the job done. Before I go much further, I want to define friendship as, simply, the relationship between two or more people who care about one another. We can take this basic definition further by adding that a true friendship often involves so much more than merely caring about another person: a lot of time and effort goes into navigating not only the good days, but also the not-so-good ones. For a friendship to be sustainable, time and effort must be given mutually and freely, and without expectation of personal benefit or return. A strong friendship is built on a foundation of honesty, trust, loyalty, and unconditional acceptance. With that said, let me introduce you to the first Amigo.

Without a Brand Ambassador, the other two Amigos would be lost, with nowhere to go and nothing to do. The Brand Ambassador is the Amigo that warmly welcomes the customer, establishes an inviting, gracious mood for their visit, and prepares the patron to be attended to by Sales and Service. Brand Ambassadors are the greeters of your company, and these employees are typically upbeat, personable, knowledgeable, and friendly. They are the most immediate representation of your company's brand. Because the Hospitality Industry includes working in hotels, restaurant, and convention centers, to name a few examples, each of these environments will inevitably take a different approach to customer service. Brand Ambassadors are hospitable people who enjoy and appreciate the art—and challenge—of creating a warm and inviting environment for their guest. They enjoy being engaged, are confident in their ability to look people in the eyes, and care about how they represent themselves. These ladies and gentlemen typically behave like—you guessed it!—ladies and gentlemen. Being a Brand Ambassador in the Hospitality Industry is about the feeling you can inspire in a customer by showing them an honest smile, a genuine desire to welcome people into your work, and a positive attitude that goes beyond service and extends to the way you treat people in general. Of course, working as a Brand Ambassador is not for everyone, and that is okay! In fact, you should be honest with yourself when you think about which of *The Three Amigos* most matches your disposition. This recognition is an important first step towards **Hitting the Sweet Spot**.

The second Amigo is Sales. Sales can effectively and precisely promise what Service will deliver. The friendship and communication between these two Amigos is integral. Sales are the wooers: you can count on them to get the contract signed. Just like a romantic relationship, Sales know how to get the ring on the finger and procure the marriage contract. Sales perform their work with a balance of product and service knowledge, a genuine sense of empathy for the customer, and the skill to know what to say and do to close the transaction. Promise only what you can deliver—but always deliver more than you promise! Sales is the Amigo most likely to face rejection—but also the one who knows how to stay motivated, move on to the next opportunity, and maintain the integrity of the product or service they sell. They know what the customer wants and are ready to give it to them.

Me, I like Sales. I say like for the simple reason that I need to believe or have a belief in what I am selling. Speaking personally, the sense of purpose I derive from Brand Ambassador is stronger. A good sales team believes in what they are selling, and it shows. Be honest with yourself!

The third Amigo is Service. Service is the final Amigo you need to know to really bring together all the lessons outlined in **Hitting the Sweet Spot**. Having highly trained service people is your company's greatest asset. Service will deliver what was promised by Sales. If Sales get the ring on the finger, Service are the folks that will keep the romance of the marriage alive. These can be your frontline and back of house staff. Everyone from chefs, cooks, servers, housekeepers, stewards, and cashiers can fall under this title. Service makes things happen—and do so according to a greater company plan or end goal. Service people are unique. Not only do they need to have knowledge of what their job entails, they also need to know the venue as both their coworkers and customers will experience it. Service involves being up-to-date with your company's marketing strategies, special events, suggested selling techniques, and community. Service people will also need to embrace the other two Amigos, Brand Ambassador and Sales. Learning from these Amigos can help Service-oriented people become more warm and friendly—even if it is a "fake it until you make it" mindset. A Sales attitude will help Service to enthusiastically promote other areas or services provided by the venue.

Knowing and respecting *The Three Amigos* can help your team reach new levels of workplace training and performance excellence. When these unique individual traits work together and employ effective communication and collaboration, an amazing customer experience is practically guaranteed. As I said before, the Amigo I most identify with is Brand Ambassador: it's my *thing*! I know, though, how important it is to have a true friendship with Sales and Service, because we all need to work together to get the job done—and to **Hit the Sweet Spot**.

I was a host—and therefore a Brand Ambassador—at the buffet, and often had to apply my understanding of *the Three Amigos* when situations such as the following occurred.

As a host, you need to learn the function and significance the different positions and duties that make up the customer's experience at the buffet. The buffet is a venue where different departments need to work seamlessly to provide amazing customer service, and a fantastic example of how to identify and work with *The Three Amigos* in a live environment. You have to perform your duties with people working for other departments, ranging from finance to front and back of house. It takes many hands to run just one location—at the buffet, five departments were needed to keep the show operational! I have also worked alongside EVS (Environmental Service or Housekeeping) and Security, to name a few other departments that came through the buffet. A lot of action can happen at any time, and you need to be ready. Knowing that you are part of a bigger picture—and what that picture looks like—can help you understand the significance of the finer details that make up your position.

To get back to the story, I had been assigned the role of greeter one evening, which involved warmly welcoming our guests, keeping the entrance foyer organized, and maintaining effective communication with my co-workers (other hosts, runners, supervisors, etc.). In this facility, overseeing the foyer was a bit of a challenge, as greeters were responsible for keeping the area clear and ensuring customer flow and safe passage through the line, and for bringing genuine, positive energy to the entire experience. Being greeter requires a great deal of patience and awareness, as well as the ability to respond to chaos with common sense, and in a grounded, calm manner. The greeter stands between two cashier stations, each usually staffed by two cashiers; to the left is a VIP line, and to the right is the regular line. After welcoming our guests, it was my job to inquire about the amount of people in their party, and then to efficiently queue the parties according to the space available in the restaurant. Being responsible for the organization of the foyer, it also fell to the greeter to be aware of the VIP line wait times, and to prioritize seating these guests.

On this very busy night, I noticed that only one cashier was working at the station for the VIP line, while two were servicing the regular line. Of course, it didn't take very long for the VIP line to become longer than the regular line, which was the last thing the company would want to happen to these valued and valuable guests. With this in mind, I asked one of the regular line's cashier if he would do me a favour.

"As you see," I said, "the VIP line is getting very long, and the customers are not feeling the love. Would you work at the VIP cash for ten to fifteen minutes to get the VIPs in?"

"Sure, Evelyn, it makes sense," was his response.

It was as easy as that! This is just a very simple example of working together as a team and focusing on the needs of the customer. Moments like these are what **Hitting the Sweet Spot** is all about.

As I mentioned in the last story, at the buffet, at least five separate departments had to operate together towards the same end. This playing field can be a challenge for some and quite simple for others. The latter is much easier to achieve when employees from every department and in every position communicate honestly and with the intention of doing their best work—for themselves *and* for their team. Interdepartmental communication is a skill that requires awareness, honest refection, and at least a little bit of common sense.

Another night at the buffet, sixty-five guests arrived in the foyer for a reservation that hadn't been communicated to the hosts. This wasn't necessarily a problem, and we had the space—what was important was making accommodations for our guests, setting up their table, and seating them as quickly as possible. I scanned the restaurant to find a place to seat the party before my coworkers and I worked together to quickly move tables, set, and assign servers. We knew what we needed to do, and we did it.

Great! Done, right?

Not by a long shot.

You can't lose your cool in a situation like this—especially with a party patiently waiting for you to get the job done. The best time to reflect on what went wrong in communicating the reservation definitely was not in the heat of the moment.

However, the greeters, servers, and hosts weren't the only ones who would be impacted by this unexpected influx. This is where big picture thinking comes in.

The next step towards **Hitting the Sweet Spot** involves going above and beyond your job duties by striving for interdepartmental excellence—in both performance and communication. In this situation, taking this step meant informing the culinary team of the large group of people coming in all at once. Bringing awareness to the Chef was paramount, and although this was not officially part of my job description, I knew that my decision would be embraced by his department. Why, you may be asking? Put simply, we were a team, and effective communication amongst every member of the team is exactly what it takes to **Hit the Sweet Spot**.

The Chef had employees under his supervision that would now need to complete more food preparation, shift their break times, and plan for the increased demand accordingly. Communicating with the heads of departments allows these decision makers to do their jobs responsibly, reliably, and confidently. It establishes a sense of trust and loyalty between departments. If the front of the house staff didn't receive notice of the reservation, it would have been senseless to assume that the back of the house staff would have known about it themselves. Having a simple conversation with your co-workers from another department which informs them of a change in plans in your department that will impact their work day is a great way to work *with* each other—and that is **Hitting the Sweet Spot!**

Analogies are a great way to illustrate an abstract concept. Even the title of this book, **Hitting the Sweet Spot**, is a figurative description of that amazing, harmonious feeling you get from a job well done—or, better yet, more than well done! I want to take a second here to drive the point home by using the analogy of a master chef in her home kitchen, whipping up a signature dish. This master chef knows more than I could ever possibly describe about cooking: she's likely to have a recipe on hand for that dish somewhere, even if she doesn't need to refer to it every time. That recipe outlines the necessary steps to be taken if the desired outcome will be achieved. **Hitting the Sweet Spot** is kind of like creating that amazing dish from the "steps" learned from the recipe, and then internalized from years of perfecting the craft. How much of an impact does the order in which ingredients are added and steps taken bear on the final taste of the meal cooking away in the pot? Sure, the answer could vary depending on what's sizzling away, but the master chef has an innate sense, drawn from experience, for when to dice, stir, turn up the heat, or add a little more spice. In the end, what makes the dish special is the magic that happens when all the ingredients are combined just right. No one element of the recipe can be considered more important than the others. Sound familiar?

I want you to think of **Hitting the Sweet Spot** the same way: it's not about prioritizing one ingredient or another, and as we turn away from *The Three Amigos* and introduce the next four chapters, it will become clear that, while the "recipe" stays the same, developing a personal sense of flair and style in your approach to making the meal will ensure that those taste buds sing every time. Consider me a "master chef" of Hospitality. I want to teach you how to make a dish named "AMAZING Customer Service." I want you to do this in your own way and reflect on your skills and disposition as you read this book. I'll give you one last piece of "cooking" advice before we put this analogy to rest—when you start stirring the pot, go clockwise, not counterclockwise. Together, we're moving forward, not backward.

To introduce and describe the four ingredients needed to create amazing customer service and **Hit the**

Sweet Spot, I'll be using personal stories and examples to illustrate how Attitude, Caring, Focus, and Responsibility influence—and can improve—the relationship you create with your customer. Each chapter is interconnected, and each story I share will be unique, with different lessons to be gleaned. Because **Hitting the Sweet Spot** is about a holistic approach to frontline service, you'll also notice that an underlying desire to provide amazing experiences to my customers in the Hospitality Industry can be traced in every anecdote. Just ask the master chef—every ingredient needs to come together to create that signature dish, so it's important not to leave anything out!

One last thing: this book is not about management. That's a project for someone else. This book is also not about tourism, politics, or navigating through workplace mind games. **Hitting the Sweet Spot** is a guide to recognizing how you can create amazing customer service for your external customers. I've learned to love it with all my heart and give my work everything that I have to offer.

I hope that, with this book, you will be able to do so too.

I have always worked in customer service, starting with McDonald's at the age of sixteen. McDonald's set the benchmark high in the fast food industry and provided a great learning opportunity for young me. That experience, and the tools I learned there, have stuck with me over the years. Working at McDonald's during my high school years not only provided me with amazing customer service training but also supported my natural skills for organizing group activities and team-building experiences to encourage workplace community and belonging. The owner gave me opportunities to organize fundraisers in a creative way, and I was so grateful for the chance to take initiative. One example was "Who's Who at McDonald's Zoo": I asked all associates and managers to bring in a baby picture and made a collage of the photos, with each assigned a unique number. Whoever brought in a photo donated $2.00 to a local charity. Then, everyone tried to name their fellow co-workers based on their baby photos, and whoever got the most right won a free value meal (I used my effective persuasion skills to entice the owner to donate a free meal—it was for charity, after all!). The fundraiser was a great way to create some fun in the workplace, give back to the community, and create goodwill in the company. I wasn't paid more to organize these initiatives. I didn't receive "Employee of the Month," either, but these incentives were totally beside the point. I did these things for *how they made me feel*. My initiatives made me happy, gave me a sense of purpose, and allowed me to create joy in a workplace for which I already felt so much gratitude.

Before I came to the casino—and after my years at McDonalds—I worked in various roles in the Hospitality Industry. I had been a hostess, server, prep cook, line cook, and seamstress prior to having the good fortune of obtaining a job at a swimming pool company, where I was employed for 13 years as a frontline associate. As I became more well-versed and familiar with my position—and with the questions our customers would most often ask—I took it upon myself to host unplanned "training" sessions in the store. When a couple would ask me about how their pool filter worked I would turn away for a moment and shout, nicely for all to hear: "Anybody need to know how their pool filter works?" More often than not, I'd save a few customers the trouble of asking the very same question that day or at a later point, and I was able to become more confident in my ability to both teach and serve. To obtain technical knowledge and to articulate that knowledge in layman terms for the customer allowed them to learn how to enjoy their investment. It was also a great gift to be able to develop the confidence to later speak in front of hundreds of people at training seminars. I am still so grateful for that opportunity. As I had at my first job, I again requested to organize, plan, and execute the company's summer picnics. It was so much fun to be creative in planning games, picking prizes, and organizing the activities for the company's workers and their families. As always, I did these things for how they made me *feel*. It was incredible to feel so happy at work, and to have a sense of purpose. I loved being able to share laughter and joy with others as I helped to create a co-operative and engaging environment for the company.

After a seven-year hiatus from working outside of my home, during which time I married and had four children, I finally landed the job of my dreams—only then, I didn't quite know it yet. As you already know, when I became a hostess at the buffet, I fell in love with my job. I loved interacting with the customers. I loved obtaining knowledge to become better-suited and trained in my role. I loved using my creativity to come up with solutions for how to improve company processes and workplace communication. I loved sharing my thoughts and ideas, regardless of whether they were going to be implemented or not. It was about being given the opportunity to think and to have a voice, as well as the freedom to use that voice in a respectful way. I loved showing my customers that I care about the way they are treated—not only by me, but by my co-workers, too. With all this love, I also learned to offer a heartfelt apology to those customers whose experiences weren't quite as satisfying: I wanted nothing more than to ensure that their experience with me was an amazing one every time.

Based on my own story, and the successes I've had along the way, I have put together four simple ingredients to get you loving what you do and **Hitting the Sweet Spot** while working in Hospitality. Frontline staff perform one of the most important jobs in any company: they are often the first employees seen by a customer, and they must know how to be direct, welcoming, and inviting in every exchange. The relationship between frontline associates and customers can make or break a company and its reputation. As we progress through **Hitting the Sweet Spot**, you'll see that this process is not just about improving "customer relations"—instead, this book encourages you to think about people and how we treat them. It's true that a company will not survive without external customers; by that same logic, the company will also not survive without its employees occupying a space where they can care for and about one another, as well as the company itself.

On that note, I want to pause here to take this opportunity to say thank you to everyone I've ever met. This book couldn't have come about without the experiences that I've had. Every person I've encountered has taught me something about who I am and what it is that I have to offer. I say thank you to every customer I've engaged with. I truly mean it.

If there is anything I have learned over the years, it is the importance of being willing to adapt. We are now in a new era of customer service: e-commerce is growing bigger every day, online banking and shopping have taken precedence… whatever service or good you can imagine, you can likely get it online. So, how do we take an old-school approach to Hospitality in the interest of making it seem new and exciting again? First, we must acknowledge that many people crave direct contact with others—and that this contact has great value.

It's in our nature: we humans enjoy togetherness. But there's also a very diverse world full of people out there. The easy customers are just that: easy. Some folks will look right at you and say, "You know what, you're amazing at this. Your smile is so bright." It's a pleasure to serve these customers because they allow me to love what I do, and they've embraced it. Of course, not everyone will make your job so simple. But **Hitting the Sweet Spot** is about bringing awareness to people at their level and inspiring them to share in the sense of joy and purpose you bring to your work.

Customer service is a two-way street. Frontline associates that exude joy will invariably be faced with customers and coworkers that are happy to let their fantasies run wild—and not always to very nice places— as to the source of your workplace happiness. If it comes down to being met with outright resistance and a bad attitude, I know that these folks have chosen not to accept what I can offer and will use their verbal and body language to try to minimize or take away what I love. I'm still thankful for these experiences, because they prove to me that, even under pressure, I can hold my head high and remember my sense of purpose, sharing myself with those who are willing to appreciate my positive, upbeat attitude. Working in a large organization, as I have done, reminds you that everyone has a different attitude about—and different experiences with—frontline service. Me, on the other hand, my joy and happiness are written all over my face. I love it. I embrace it. I feel almost like a politician, shaking hands, smiling, and catching up with the people around me. I've met many people in my years of work that have simply marveled at my attitude.

"How do you do it? How do you get there?" These are the questions these people typically ask when they realize how deep my love for Hospitality runs. Well, that's what **Hitting the Sweet Spot** is about. This book is a response to anyone who has ever challenged me to reaffirm my dedication to be a Brand Ambassador by telling me, "You're crazy, Evelyn." For anyone who has ever worked in an environment and believed that they are only a number, and that their company doesn't care about their passion: that way of thinking will only foster negative outcomes. Attitude is so important. The language that you use when face-to-face with fellow associates, regardless of where they are on the company ladder, can directly impact the social culture of your workplace. Every person you encounter needs support to become inspired, and to believe in themselves and their ability to **Hit the Sweet Spot**, too. Encourage this growth, because everyone is unique and will flourish in their own way. Don't take it away. Don't minimize. Strive to **Hit the Sweet Spot** together.

I'm here to inspire others, and to bring awareness to how our individual behaviours and language can affect our interpersonal relationships—for the better. As frontline associates, we are not numbers. We occupy a significant role in the company and develop strong bonds with our customers. If "I'm just another one of many" is or has been your mentality, this book can help you revisit and change this way of thinking. Along the way, you'll discover what you need to prosper and feel satisfied and joyous in the Hospitality Industry.

I'm going to wrap this Introduction up with a brief anecdote about writing this book and desiring some guidance and direction. I'm currently studying psychology in university, so I decided to touch base with one of my professors about attitude, one of the four "ingredients" in this book. What can I say about attitude? —that's what I wanted to know. As I shared some of my stories with my professor, and recounted my intentions for the book, she started to warmly laugh. She told me, "Evelyn, your energy is beautiful. You're able to articulate what it is that you want. Your stories are fabulous. I think your greatest skill or challenge that you're going to face is being focused on the topic at hand. Because I think you have about 20 books inside of you."

And she's right, of course. When you love the Hospitality Industry the way I do, it's hard for your fond memories not to blur into one another. But this isn't a nostalgic memoir. What I've compiled here is a more focused and comprehensive guide to a very tangible outcome—**Hitting the Sweet Spot**. Just like frontline associate crossing paths with managers, customers, executives, coworkers, and so on, this book will teach you how to adapt and flourish in any situation involving *The Three Amigos* and Hospitality. Interrelated though these chapters may be, the end goal requires all four "ingredients" for their own unique characteristics. In a similar way, we can all **Hit the Sweet Spot** when we are willing to come together and relate to one another with respect for each person's individuality and what they have to offer.

Chapter 1

Attitude

"The only keeper of your happiness is you.

Stop giving people power to control your

smile, your worth and your attitude."

—*Mandy Hale*

HAVING A POSITIVE ATTITUDE towards your customer benefits you and the company you work for. I will share with you that I am a positive person by nature. I see life as a beautiful journey of learning and welcoming new ways of thinking and being. When anyone asks me "How are you?" my response will always be, "I am amazing!" This is not self-affirmation; I am speaking with the intention of reflecting on and understanding my actions and my values. It is not that everything in my life is amazing—I just don't have to finish the sentence! I could be amazingly tired, or amazingly bored, or amazingly busy. It doesn't matter. I only say *I am amazing* and leave it at that. I look at the beauty in life, and at how unexpected events can be seen as opportunities rather than problems. Of course, for some people this disposition can be annoying, and, of course, a positive attitude often just doesn't come naturally for everyone.

Ask yourself, and be honest, are you a positive person? Do you like the Hospitality Industry and its values? What goals would like to achieve while working in the Hospitality Industry? When approached with a new way of thinking, as you will be in this book, you might find yourself wondering how this perspective benefits you. Well, I am so happy to answer this question. Would you like to grow within the company? Having a positive attitude can improve your earnings, whether through an increase in tips or an advancement within your company.

There are many opportunities to grow in the Hospitality Industry if you are willing to open your mind to a new way of thinking which encourages you to believe that having a positive attitude will help you to find the satisfaction and fulfilment you should be able to gain from your workplace. If status or a promotion are not your goals, don't worry: having a positive attitude can also allow you to develop a set of social skills that you can take with you in any company or sector you work for. Having a positive attitude gives you opportunities to create amazing teams to get the job done with trust, loyalty, and teamwork. It also benefits you physically. Positive people feel good about themselves and it shows on the outside.

To hit the **Sweet Spot**, you will need to do some basic self-reflection to focus on how YOU represent you. This process starts with evaluating your attitude.

If you are blessed with children, or if you have children in your life, you know that you can see right away that a child's attitude will be written all over his or her face. Yes, facial expression is your first go-to when it comes to understanding attitude: it is the clearest, and often the most primary, indication of your feelings. There is nothing more beautiful than the smile that emanates from the eyes of someone with a positive attitude, because this disposition radiates from within. The other indicators are physical and aural cues such as body language, tone of voice, verbal style, and verbal content. **Hitting the Sweet Spot** starts with you, and with understanding how you show your own emotions to your internal (coworkers, etc.) and external customers. So, with that in mind, let's go over some of the common facial expressions.

Joy can be seen in the eyes. Sharing your smile with a joyful customer can create an amazing experience in which both of your positive attitudes are mutually supported and encouraged. On the other hand, you can easily take away from a customer's happiness by not returning their enthusiasm: be mindful of the energy you are receiving from your customer and do your best to always express yourself politely and warmly through both your words and your facial expression. If you can maintain a positive disposition and find joy in your work, you will feel better about and more invested in your place in the company and the relationships you form with your internal and external customers.

An honest smile has many benefits when it comes to your work as a frontline employee: you are more attractive to people when you smile and appear more approachable to internal and external customers. An honest smile is contagious, and it makes others feel happy and comfortable to be around you. An honest smile draws people towards you, and as a frontline employee, it is your job to be comfortable with this attention while also servicing your customers. An honest smile also shows that you are a positive person and has a positive approach to your job and life. This approach will help you in the s-good times.

Many of us who work in frontline service have mixed feelings about general customer interactions. On one hand we want and need them. Without customers we don't have a job! But I often find myself hoping that I'll only have to interact with nice customers because I won't have to work too hard to make them happy. Interesting dilemma, wouldn't you say?

I am going to tell it like it is: it is *not* your customer's job to make *your* day. It is, however, *your* job to make your customer's day. This is the Hospitality Industry in a nutshell.

We are all given opportunities to make the not-so-good times better if we are mindful of how we represent ourselves. There are, of course, facial expressions other than joy that you can look for to help guide you in understanding yourself and others. The happy customer is the easy customer, so how do we understand the emotions of the not-so-easy customer?

From my experience, sometimes the most challenging interactions are the most rewarding in the long run. Let's go over how to recognize some of these challenges and reflect on how to overcome them.

Are you an angry Elf on the Shelf? You can't change what you don't acknowledge. Be honest with yourself. Do you get angry? Are you a thrower, or a table banger? Or maybe you tend to raise your voice or use fear and intimidation to get what you want?

I will say that, in my personal experiences, anger is an emotion that can quickly escalate to acts of violence. It takes an emotionally strong person not to meet anger with anger. Be self-aware of how you are representing YOU. In the Hospitality Industry, if you are prone to emotional displays, you will not last long. If you don't see yourself resolving this disposition through honest self-reflection, you should consider a different industry or profession.

Giving in to your anger is not acceptable in the Hospitality Industry. However, after saying that, dealing with and having the emotional control to defuse anger in a customer or coworker is a skill of paramount importance.

Like joy, anger can also be identified in the eyes: an intense glare usually accompanied by tightened lips. You know: that one look that your parents gave you when they were not-so-happy with you. When faced with an angry customer, stay calm and listen patiently to their needs. Allow the customer the freedom to express their emotions without immediately trying to offer an explanation. Repeat back to the customer what you think you heard for confirmation. Maintain eye contact and show that you understand their situation and you will do the best you can to remedy their concerns. Apologize for yourself or on behalf of another employee, if need be. It is important to put the customer first and to respect their perspective of the situation. Taking a step back to think about their experience and their needs is a great way to turn the issue into an opportunity to develop empathy and work towards defusing the problem at hand.

Sharing A Story

How You Make the Customer Feel

Let me share a story with you regarding an angry customer who once gave me the chance to resolve a potential blow-up. In this story, you'll see that being mindful and having a positive attitude can make a not-so-good experience an amazing one.

The section I was serving at the buffet had closed for the evening and I was doing my side duties of cleaning the busing station, stocking cutlery, filling salt and pepper shakers, and preparing to reset my tables. I was approached by my supervisor if I would reopen my section because there was an unexpected line after the theatre letting out and no tables were available for seating. I said yes, and the hosts immediately began seating my section. In this restaurant, the servers were responsible for setting the tables with cutlery while the host's job was to seat customers, direct them to the buffet and inform them that their server will be arrive in a moment. Because of the sudden influx of customers, my section was seated all at once. I saw the chaos as a challenge: in my mind, it is all about the customer, and having a customer seated is more important than having them waiting for a table at the front of the restaurant. Unfortunately, with everything happening so quickly, a party of six returned to their table with food from the buffet before I was able to bring them cutlery, and one guest became frustrated.

"Where are our knives and forks? Do you think we're a bunch of animals?" I heard as I was approaching the table.

"I am very sorry about not having your cutlery ready for you," I replied.

I proceeded to set the table, but the guest was still clearly frustrated about not already having her cutlery.

"This is just horrible, we come here for a nice evening and have a wonderful meal, and this is what we deal with," she said.

I stayed very calm and took the time to kneel in front of our guest to communicate more directly. I looked her in the eyes and said calmly, but kindly,

"My name is Evelyn and I am your server. I do apologize for not having the table set. If there is anything that you need to make this evening an amazing one, just ask for me, and I will do everything in my power to make it so. Please enjoy your meal."

I waited for her response before I stood up. All she said was, "Thank you, Evelyn."

After this exchange, the rest of the evening was a wonderful engagement, and the party of six were beautiful people. The customer that had been frustrated about the table setting later apologized for her behaviour and handed me a $20 bill as a tip. In response I said, "Thank you, that is very nice of you. I hope the rest of your evening here will be amazing."

How we make the customer *feel* is the cornerstone of **Hitting the Sweet Spot**. I took the time to listen to a frustrated customer, and to allow her the space to get out what she was feeling, before I took responsibility to make it right.

In the Hospitality Industry we are given moments of choice. I could have chosen to direct the energy to the host for not helping me set the tables. I could have chosen to complain about the customer and ignore her negative attitude towards me. What I chose was to maintain my positive attitude towards this situation and see how I could make it better for everyone—and I received a $20 tip for that awareness!

Beautiful! I love it when you **Hit the Sweet Spot**.

Please know that when we understand the difference between our own emotions and the reasons why we get angry, we are also given the opportunity to recognize these tendencies in others. Anger is not the same thing as frustration. Frustration can lead to anger, which itself can be accompanied by an intention to cause bodily harm. However, frustration can often be resolved by trying to understand what the customer *perceives* to be right, and then doing your best to make it so.

I am very fortunate to have no story for you about handling an angry customer that wished to cause me bodily harm. Most of you will deal with frustrated customers, not angry ones, and understanding how to recognize the difference between the two will guide you greatly as a frontline professional. After saying that, the escalation from frustration to anger can happen very quickly if you are not mindful of your own responses. A great deal of humility is needed to **Hit the Sweet Spot**. If you recognize that you may not be willing to strive towards this level of self-awareness, you may want to ask yourself, *why are you in the Hospitality Industry, and what do you hope to personally achieve from working in this sector?*

The Internal Customer

I worked in an organization that provided uniforms for their employees. The powers that be made the decisions about the design, material, and the number of uniforms that would be given to each employee. You may have already guessed that I felt grateful for what I was given. I said thank you, as I do when I am given anything for "$Free.99": to me, it's the only thing that can be said! I didn't have to pay out of pocket for these uniforms, and if something didn't fit properly, there was even a seamstress on hand to alter it. The company wanted you to feel comfortable in your uniform.

Now, on the other hand, some of my coworkers saw the situation differently. "I don't like the colour"; "I don't like the material"; "I don't like..." you can fill in the blank. You might think back to the "nutshell" version of the Hospitality Industry I mentioned earlier: add to the list that it is not your company's job to please their employees with the uniform. It is, however, part of your job to wear a uniform, and to uphold their brand in doing so. The company was kind enough to offer so many amenities to ensure their employees' comfort; in return, these employees are simply asked to wear the uniform they have been freely provided. What others perceive as bumps in the road can also be a matter of simple attitude adjustment: you may not enjoy wearing a uniform, but can you feel grateful for these services, especially for the wonderful cost of $Free.99?

Putting It on Paper

Put your energy on the positive by concentrating on the things you are grateful for from your employer. Write down a list of things that you are grateful for at your workplace. Some examples might include pay, benefits, social events, flexible hours, the industry itself, or the venue.

1. _____

2. _____

3. _____

4. _____

5. _____

6. _____

7. _____

8. _____

9. _____

10. _____

Now, write a list of things that you are grateful for from the people you work *with*, including your co-workers, supervisors, managers, etc.

1. _____

2. _____

3. _____

4. _____

5. _____

6. _____

7. _____

8. _____

9. _____

10. _____

Finally, write out a list of the lessons you have learned and value from your workplace or your experience in the Hospitality Industry.

1. _____

_____

2. _____

_____

3. _____

_____

4. _____

_____

5. _____

_____

6. _____

_____

7. _____

_____

8. _____

_____

9. _____

_____

10. _____

_____

Now, read over these three lists, and take the time to reflect on why what you have written is important to you.

Try to remember this feeling during the not-so-good times.

This story is about attitude and how to be aware of it as it regards our internal customers. When we can reflect on ourselves in this way, we can also extend awareness to our external customers.

At the buffet, servers and hosts worked together as a team. One day, I overheard a troubling comment as I walked into the bussing station. The topic of discussion was a new hire and how incompetent she apparently was. I didn't make a comment to my coworker about how rude it was to say these things. Instead, I asked her a question. I simply said, "So, I'm just curious. How long have you been a server?"

"All my life, 30 years, all I've ever done is serve," she replied.

"So, you have a lot of experience being a server?" I asked.

"Yeah, I do."

"And how long have you worked here?" I inquired.

"Almost ten years."

"Wow, that's a long time. So, you know a lot about what this job entails, you know how to find whatever it is you need to perform your job, you know the process, and you're very familiar with the ins and outs of how this works."

"Yeah, I really do. I know a lot," she said.

I said, "How long has the new hire worked here?"

"Two weeks," she responded.

"What a difference! Why don't we give her a little bit more time to catch up? Why not share with her what you know because she doesn't have the experience just yet?"

With this comment, I was able to provide insight to my coworker without being rude or passive aggressive, without agreeing with her, and without conforming to her attitude (which was not necessarily wrong—I think that she just needed a reminder about the importance of awareness). Often, people are not even fully aware of the potential impact of comments that they make in passing.

"Thank you, Evelyn, for bringing that to my awareness," she said. I knew from her response that she had answered her own questions, and that I had enabled her to recognize her own attitude about those around her, which are both so important when **Hitting the Sweet Spot**.

We really do want to watch our attitude, not only about ourselves, but also about the people we work around and with. Share knowledge and check your attitude. Allow people time to learn. They're not going to learn if you're not sharing what you know. New hires will inevitably find training more difficult if they are made to feel inadequate by those who have been in frontline service for thirty years.

Give them some time. Give them some space. Encourage them. Inspire them. Motivate them to work hard and get to where you are. **Hitting the Sweet Spot** is about raising the bar of self-awareness and knowing that it will benefit you personally, whether by developing more meaningful relations with your internal and external customers, generating financial growth, or improving your attitude towards your work and your company. Strive to give everyone you encounter a positive representation of who you are.

As a frontline associate in Hospitality, my own personal experience is that an awareness of body language, voice, and verbal style will help you as you find the **Sweet Spot**. When you are **Hitting the Sweet Spot**, your attitude will reflect it. Challenge yourself to always be aware of your own verbal style, body language, and tone of voice. It is powerful for you, as an individual, to see yourself honestly, and to understand the energy that you give to your external and internal customer.

Ask yourself, and be honest: do you like people? If you don't, how can we shift your way of thinking to at least get you through each day with a more positive outlook? Be mindful of the things you say to and about your customer, yourself, and others. Language is important and creating a positive internal dialogue with yourself about your work is a great place to start.

Chapter 2

Care

"...People will forget what you said, people will forget what you did, but people will never forget how you made them feel."

—Maya Angelou

EMPATHY FOR OTHERS IS ONE OF THE hardest assets to harness. We are living in a world that seems to reward the self-oriented, and we tend to look at our own mistakes as flaws, rather than *miss-takes*. But we are always capable of doing better, regardless of what has come before. When you understand and practice empathy towards yourself and others, you will lead a more fulfilling and healthier life.

How does one go about teaching and prioritizing empathy as a frontline employee? Empathy is something that you do with an open mind and heart and as you are doing it, you *feel* it. Empathy is a verb, an ACTION. Customer empathy is what creates the warm, fuzzy feeling you get when you return to a business and they remember your name and are pleased you've come back, or when they are obviously interested in you as a person. Let's explore how to develop empathy to better serve your customers.

Using your *ears:* listen for what is not being said. Hearing the tone of voice and type of language being used will guide you when what you are hearing is different than what your customer is truly feeling.

Using your *eyes:* be mindful of the body while speaking with your customer. Create a baseline of how they are reacting. Do you see eye-rolling? Is he or she making a fist, or shaking their head "no" but saying "yes"? People are talking to you more than you think.

Empathy is the ability to sense other people's emotions in conjunction with imagining what someone else might be thinking or feeling. How is this helpful for you in the Hospitality Industry? Developing empathy for your customers will provide the customer with an experience of *feeling* the service rather than just receiving it.

Being in the Hospitality Industry gives you opportunities to engage with many different demographics and environments. Having an open mind to learn *about* people will give you an appreciation *for* people. Hospitality involves developing an *intimate* relationship with your customer, as well as learning about and embracing cultures different from your own.

Hold on. Let's not get our knickers in a bunch. True intimacy is on a higher level, beyond the physical, which most think of when thinking of intimacy. Let's take a close look at the word *intimacy* and break down how it can be related to benefiting you as a frontline professional.

The word intimacy when said very quickly is *In-To-Me-See*.

When you put yourself in another person's shoes, without losing your sense of self in the process, you create an *In-To-Me-See feeling* of understanding for the customer. *In-To-Me-See* is a state of vulnerability, which can be challenging for some to understand and appreciate. *In-To-Me-See* involves seeing the person in front of you as an individual with unique qualities and seeing them from the inside out.

Why is this important as a frontline professional?

This is a very good question. To answer that question for yourself means developing a growth mindset. With a growth mindset, people believe that they can develop their basic abilities through dedication and hard work. People are inspired to challenge their perceived limitations through their love of learning, and to use resilience to accomplish amazing things.

Applying this mindset in a business culture gives associates the opportunity to recognize what they are truly capable of doing, and to create *In-To-Me-See* experiences for their customers. Companies that embrace a growth mindset for the entire organization (bottom up and top down) are supporting collaboration across organizational boundaries and not just between units or individual employees. These organizations have a commitment to mastering these valuable skills regardless of individual moods, with the understanding that passion and purpose come from doing great work, which comes from expertise and experience. A growth mindset involves always pushing into unfamiliar territory to build employee confidence through the art of learning new things, challenging current limitations, and developing natural skills. With a growth mindset you can see what you need to do to reach where it is that you want to be—without letting setbacks influence your determination to keep moving forward. A company with a growth mindset will acknowledge these obstacles and join forces with their team to get creative and build on individual skills to obtain the desired outcome. In other words, a growth mindset embraces the creative process, encourages a cognitive approach, and allows information to flow freely throughout the company.

How will you know if your company cares about its employees and customers in this way?

You will know if a company cares by how they treat their employees, and by the culture of the company more generally. Canada and the United States operate on an older working mantra of standardization. Standardization was developed in the 1800s for manufacturing. It is a chain of command approach, which prioritizes individual departments operating separately. Fear and intimidation is valued: you go through the chain of command or else. In contrast, **Hitting the Sweet Spot** advocates embracing a holistic approach to frontline work in which balance is created through the recognition and inclusion of our friends, *The Three Amigos*, and the values that support their work.

In-To-Me-See is also culturally important for your organization. We are facing a shift in the way we see our leaders. The "do as I say, not as I do" mindset is rapidly changing with the #MeToo movement and very powerful figures are being exposed. The logic of *absolute power corrupts absolutely* is thankfully being replaced with one of *I will do better by respecting my fellow human beings, and by being aware of and honest about the impact of the deeds that I perform.* Leaders now understand not to live life looking over their shoulders, but instead to live in the NOW by acknowledging how their words, actions, and behaviours will affect them and those that they lead in the future. Be mindful of the leaders within your company, and in your Human Resources department. An organization with weak HR likely has weak leaders, and weak leadership is reflected in poor communication, micromanagement, and intimidation.

How can you as a frontline professional create an *In-To-Me-See* experience for your customer?

You start with a heartfelt welcome. Welcoming your customers creates a *feeling* of appreciation. To me, Hospitality is having wanting, valuing, and appreciating everyone who enters my workplace. Yes, I know that some customers can be more challenging than others to welcome. But we teach people how to behave, don't we? The squeaky wheel gets oiled. I have the mindset, "It is nice to feel important, but it more important to be nice," when dealing with "the squeaky wheel." Thankfully, these customers are few and far between, especially if your company has developed and implemented structure to achieve growth.

Caring

I would like to share with you a story about Caring for a customer, guiding you in through an *In-To-Me-See* experience.

A wonderful older lady came to the buffet alone one day. I could tell by her mannerisms and way of holding herself that something wasn't quite right, although I couldn't put my finger on what it was. She was well dressed and looked well taken care of. Her clothing was high-end, and her hair and makeup were elegant and refined. She reminded me of my mother with her disposition and her style, and her demeanor intrigued me. I approached her and asked if there was anything I could do for her? She informed me she was waiting for her husband. He hadn't come to the restaurant to meet her yet. She wanted to wait for a little while longer for her husband to arrive.

During this engagement, I observed her mannerisms, her speech, her direct eye contact; I knew that there was something off, something not quite right. Again, I was not one hundred percent sure what it could be, and the restaurant was very busy with a lineup, so I kept my eye on her. Eventually, I offered her a chair to be more comfortable. After twenty minutes I asked her again if she still wanted to wait for her husband and she said, in the softest voice, "No, I'm going to go have dinner. I can't wait for my husband. I'm very hungry and I need to eat something."

She expressed how very nervous she was to go in and eat without her husband. "If you like," I told her, "I'll keep you company for a while." I asked her name and the name of her husband.

"My name is Sue and my husband is John," she informed me.

"Ok, Sue, let's go get you a table and something to eat, shall we? I'll keep an eye on you and make sure you're okay."

Sue asked me my name, to which I responded, "My name is Evelyn and I am here to service you Sue."

"I really like you, Evelyn," Sue said.

My reply was, "And I really like you."

Sue held my arm as we walked into the restaurant, and as we were walking I again had the feeling that something was not right. Sue expressed her concern about having dinner without her husband, how big the restaurant was, and how nervous the situation made her.

There were red flags in her dialogue that allowed me to notice that something was missing. I wanted to keep an eye on Sue because I cared about her wellbeing and didn't want anyone to take advantage of her. The restaurant was in a gaming facility and even the most alert person can be a target for unwanted attention. I wanted Sue to not feel nervous or scared, so I brought her to a table and I sat down with her for a few minutes. I informed my coworker that I would be with this person for a little bit and I let my supervisor know that there's something just not quite right and I would like to try to help her. I am grateful that the facility encouraged and supported their employees to *care* about their customers. I was able to see that Sue was very nervous to sit at the restaurant and eat by herself. She didn't want to give her drink order to the server that came to the table, and she would only talk to me. I created trust with Sue to feel safe with me, and she needed that. I also was mindful that I couldn't stay with her the whole time, and that she needed to find her husband or caregiver in this very large restaurant in a very large casino. I went with her to get some food and was able to sit down and started to get some information now that she felt comfortable and more relaxed. Sue felt comfortable in telling me her full name and her husband's name to see if we could find and get in touch with him.

It's all about taking the time and being mindful of who needs extra attention. When you are aware, there are clues you can look for. I informed my supervisor of the information I had obtained, and I asked her if she could contact the appropriate department to see if there was a way that we could locate her husband. It's all about taking the time to care about your customers. I am pleased to announce that we found Sue's husband, and that Sue herself had a wonderful experience; in fact, she even wanted to give me a tip. *In-To-Me-See* is a team effort that made the outcome of this experience an amazing one. Before leaving the restaurant, Sue said, "You are a very beautiful woman," and I said, "Thank you, as are you. Please enjoy the rest of your visit."

When you love what you do, it is easy to create moments of *In-To-Me-See* for others without fear, without judgment, without jealousy, but instead with a willingness to help.

Being successful in the Hospitality Industry is about having an awareness of others' needs while also treating them kindly and with courtesy and gratitude. I am a huge fan of entertaining people and of Hospitality in my own home. Having people in my home is my greatest joy. I also love watching *Downton Abbey* by Masterpiece, which is about the interaction of the Lord of the mansion and the servers that work there. When I host people at work and at home, I wholeheartedly embrace the mindset that the show wishes to portray: "to serve with honour and pride in your profession."

I hold these words close to my heart. I strive to serve with honour and pride in my profession in the Hospitality Industry and demonstrate my care for others by tapping into a feeling of graciousness.

A repeat customer with whom I had created a rapport came into a restaurant I worked in one day. I greeted him as I have always greeted him, with an honest smile from my eyes. I knew this man over the years from being his host and taking him to his table. We had an amicable relationship and I knew where he enjoyed sitting. That day, as we proceeded to walk to his table, I said, "How nice it is to see you!" and took his arm as we walked. The restaurant had amazing views and the day was warm, bright and clear. I mentioned how beautiful the weather was and suggested that he would benefit from a walk outside. He was always so warm, and often shared a smile with me. When I said this, I turned to look at him and out of the blue, looking into my eyes, he said, "I could fuck you right now."

Without missing a beat, I maintained his eye contact and said, "We both know that you don't mean it. Let's go to your table."

We continued to his table and I wished him a good day.

It was very disappointing to have this man, who I had trusted, look at me in that manner. It was disappointing to be spoken to in this way when I had done nothing to encourage it.

Having the awareness to tap into a sense of graciousness without feeling the need to take any further action is a skill that should be valued in the Hospitality Industry. To create the fine balance of being friendly without crossing that boundary, and to respond and act in a gracious way to inappropriate language is challenging. This gentleman, after he had his meal, waited for me at the front of the restaurant to offer an apology. He allowed me to express my concern that his behaviour was wrong and said, "I would totally understand if you had slapped me in the face. It was very inappropriate what I said, and I apologize. I thank you for not slapping me."

"You didn't mean it and it doesn't change anything. You have a great day and I will always look forward to seeing you," I responded.

Unfortunately, I never saw him again, but I knew that in that moment I didn't need to overreact to someone else's inappropriate behaviour. Have control and allow people the benefit of the doubt; use graciousness to defuse an otherwise very unfortunate outcome.

Your care can be seen in how represent yourself to your customers. Care is also about allowing an opportunity for your internal customers to become aware of their actions with the use of humour. Humour is singular in nature. Are you open-minded with a quick wit? Humour is challenging for the simple reason that not everyone will always be on the same page about what they find funny. Having a sense of humour is having wit, banter and seeing life's silliness. The challenge in frontline service will be knowing when a joke has crossed the line and become a form of inappropriate banter.

One day, I was coming out of an elevator and overheard a conversation between two younger male co-workers. The conversation was evidently not private, as the two men were loud enough for everyone to hear. I soon came upon the one young man teasing his co-worker.

"What are you spending all your money on, working two jobs... prostitutes?"

I looked at the second young man and I teasingly said, "You never need to pay for a prostitute. Ask a nice girl out for dinner and treat her right. Become friends and create a relationship... then you will find what you are looking for. A nice young man like yourself would never need to pay for a prostitute."

Well, to my surprise, this young man looked at me and said, "I'd pay for you."

"Oh, really?" I responded, and quickly removed my smile. "Well, now. I am going to think about what you just said to me and I am going to come back and let you know if it was an insult or a compliment."

I turned and walked away. Working in the Hospitality Industry for many years you have a way of understanding people, boys and girls, men and women. This young man is just that—*young*—and for me to overreact to a comment I felt was harmlessly intentioned by going to a supervisor, manager, or directly to Human Resources would have little to no value for anyone. The cost to the company, the time lost, and the stress alone can feel energy draining. So, this is how I created awareness for lasting change, because I did feel in this case that the young man would remember my reaction more deeply than any trip to HR or possible job loss. A few hours later I approached him and said, with a smile, "I have had some time to consider what you said earlier, and I have decided that the insult or compliment will lay in the amount that you are willing to pay."

The young man sighed with relief said. "Anything, anything you want."

I gave him a high five and we laughed. I also said to him, "You are a nice young man and I thank you for thinking that I am attractive in that way. Being a wife and a mother of four, it is flattering, if you want to believe that or not. I would prefer that you would think of me in a respectful way instead. Please be mindful of the things you are saying to people. If you had said that to someone else, you could be in a lot of trouble right now."

Creating an awareness that this man could choose to respond differently in these situations through humour and graciousness gave him an opportunity to understand to behave better in the future, and to achieve growth rather than be met with punishment. This young man treated me with respect from that point on, as I did him.

Chapter 3

Focus

"If you would plant for days, plant flowers. If you would plant for years, plant trees. If you would plant for eternity, plant ideas!"

—*Proverb*

THE FOCUS I AM GOING TO DISCUSS IN this chapter is about more than carefully deciding the steps needed to see the task at hand through to completion. Focus, as I see it, is what gives you the sense of patience and purpose needed to "plant for eternity," rather than for days. What distinguishes focus from obligation is a mentality of *inspiration*, rather than a mere sense of *motivation*; in the workplace, tapping into the former, rather than falling into the latter, can be difficult.

So many heroic characters act from a place of *inspiration*: he or she *chooses* to act within their capabilities to do something positive or selfless for another person or the community. Villains and antagonists, on the other hand, often display what I describe here as *motivation*: these folks feel that they *must* do something with their skills and abilities, but the ideal outcome of this action is to achieve a specific goal, rather than to act in the service of another.

Inspiration flourishes when you have a sense of purpose, and work with love, joy, and compassion. It is not about competition: instead, you genuinely wish to learn, grow, and execute tasks to be more personable while also increasing your value to the company. *Motivation*, in contrast, can be seen in those who desire and act in the interest of gaining power, status, or external rewards. Unlike *inspiration*, those with a motive tend to compete for the sake of besting their peers, impressing their superiors, or gaining favorable reputation or treatment from others.

To **Hit the Sweet Spot**, your focus needs to come from a place of inspiration, not motivation. Nothing can stop you from "planting for eternity" when you are truly inspired. Reflecting on what drives you to do your best work is a good way to get in touch with what you need to do to feel more *inspired*, not *motivated*, to be where you want to be. While this may sound abstract, there are a few practical matters you can address along the way to deeper self-reflection.

Develop a Sense of Intention

In a very literal way, keeping focused at work is necessary for you to perform your job more efficiently and effectively. Distractions big and small can draw your focus away from what you need to accomplish while on the clock. When you arrive at your workplace, you should do so with a sense of intention: understand not only *why* you are there (the money alone is a good answer here!), but also *why* your unique capabilities and circumstances have lead you here, to the Hospitality Industry, where you have the opportunity to interact with new people every day and make a major impact on their journey.

Keep this intention in mind as you go about your day. When you are aware of yourself and what is expected of you, you can use this sense of focus to recognize the potential distractions that may affect your focus at work.

Use Your Intention to Pay Attention

Paying attention is about staying present. Being present is best achieved by tapping into your senses and using them to wholeheartedly engage with your surroundings. Having a strong sense of purpose will make it easier for you to recognize and think holistically about your workplace as a constantly shifting environment with which you must keep up. At any moment, the dynamic between your environment, your patrons, and your coworkers can totally change. When times get tough and you need to maintain grace under fire, being present and aware of these shifting relationships through focus will make all the difference.

You can develop your awareness by tapping into the foundation provided for you by the senses. If you can see, both your immediate and peripheral vision may allow you to focus intently on the person in front of you while also being conscious of your surroundings. Being seen might not be *your* favourite pastime, but you can create a moment of real *In-To-Me-See* for your coworkers and patrons when you use your literal focus to carve out a "small picture" moment in a "big picture" environment.

You also need to be aware of the safety and accessibility of your workplace. Listen closely, if you can, not only to the conversation at hand, but also to the tone used in your exchanges. Listen for sounds that might be out of place or indicative of a health and safety issue. Your senses of touch, taste, and smell can also be of paramount importance here, especially in the Food and Beverage industry: from a firm handshake to a meal that apparently doesn't taste quite right or a smell that seems like a sign of trouble, if you are aware of your surroundings, you can also be aware of how to **Hit the Sweet Spot** within them by staying on top of any challenge that may arise.

Workplace Distractions

What distracts you may not be an issue for others, but being present and focused is as much about having a strong sense of empathy and *inspiration* for long-term improvement, success, and sustainability as it is about ensuring that you can do a good job while you're at work each day.

Here, you'll find examples of distractions that may nibble at your focus in the workplace. Remember to reflect on your thoughts about each item listed: if you are inclined to dismiss something because it doesn't seem to relate to your experience, take a second to understand how and why this factor may distract someone else.

Coworkers	*Environment*	*Management*
Gossip	Lighting	Human Resources
Friendships and Romantic Relationships	Location	Schedules
Mobile Phones	Time of Day	Expectations
Personal Lives	Temperature	Break Policies
Workplace Disagreements	Decorations and Ambience	Interpersonal Relationships

There's no denying that your home life will have an impact on your work life. Some folks seem to have mastered the work-life balance while others have adopted the "what happens at work, stays at work" (or home, for that matter) mentality. **Hitting the Sweet Spot** is about redefining the relationship between these two seemingly separate parts of life and fostering a sense of *inspiration* towards being aware of your personal life and values as a means of improving your sense of self and self-awareness.

Understanding work-life balance involves fostering an awareness that your home life is in harmony. Your relationship with your partner, if you have one, is healthy, committed, and mutually supportive. All members of the home treat each other with respect and can communicate freely. In other words, there is peace: no distractions from your home life will spill over into your work life when this harmony has been achieved. Problems in your personal life or in your relationships should be dealt with in your personal time and space, not at work. In the same way, your relationships at work should also be healthy, making up a harmonious environment in which you can feel comfortable addressing the issues that may occur during the work day with the appropriate parties. In other words, when you achieve this harmony, you will not need to bring up your issues about home at work, or vice versa. Your focus will improve because of this effort.

My perspective on establishing a work-life balance has always meant not trying to hold myself too strictly to allotting hours for one task or the other, because the demands of both work and home may fluctuate at any time. It's important to be flexible as well as focused. Depending on your position and the responsibilities that comprise your job, you may be required to travel, or to finish a big project during the hours outside of the work day, which may involve working late evenings, weekends or holidays. Understanding your work responsibilities and establishing what these duties will entail with your partner can foster trust, respect, and a willingness to be more supportive of one another's professional pursuits. A harmonious home life provides a foundation for bringing focus and present to your work to get the job done. If peace at home is not the case for you, bringing awareness to any issues that may distract your attention from work is a key step toward having them resolved. **Hitting the Sweet Spot** is that very special moment when you're happily running to work and then happily running home, because balance, peace, and harmony have been created and maintained in both spaces.

One challenging "personal" distraction in the workplace is romance. Yes, let's have a conversation about the elephant in the room. Love happens, and it is a beautiful thing. I believe in love with all my heart. The challenge here lies in sustaining a healthy workplace relationship between two single people. What happens if things don't go well? It also may be the case that, as in some situations, when their home lives are out of balance, people look to their workplace connections for comfort and acceptance rather than dealing with these issues in their own space. Consciously or unconsciously, not having your personal life in balance will not only affect your job performance but can also indirectly influence unwanted attention (or attraction) from seemingly friendly coworkers.

If you find yourself in this situation, a way to gauge whether the attention you are receiving from a coworker has broken boundaries is through the "Friendship Test." A respectful workplace friend will agree to meet and create social occasions for spouses or partners to attend (if you have one). The intention here is to build respectful workplace relationships. If a co-worker is not interested in meeting or having a social interaction with your spouse, chances are that his or her intention is different than yours. I would recommend trying to recognize these behaviours prior to investing your time and energy into workplace friendships.

Our health, home, family, personal expectations, and self-esteem will undoubtedly have an impact on the way we see ourselves as unique individuals, as coworkers, as peers, as friends, and so on. However, when you arrive at work, its's time to park your personal life in the garage and close the door. We all have lives outside of work. Our personal life is just that, personal. Having the ability to handle your personal distractions on your own time can be very difficult and at the same time very rewarding. *

Being aware of how you are feeling is half the battle, and it isn't always easy to get in touch with difficult emotions. Are you angry about Mr. Right slowly turning into Mr. Wrong? Are the kids not helping around the house, making you feel unappreciated or used? Not so

---

* There are some things that you should obtain professional help with, such as losing a loved one, divorce, custody issues, and so on. You know you best. Seek and ask for the help you need and remember that you can "plant for eternity" within yourself, too.

happy with the police officer that gave you a speeding ticket on the way to work, because the former Mr. Right didn't do the shopping like he promised? Did the paving company, hired on the strength of a recommendation by a co-worker, not do the job you wished (and paid) for?

There are so many potential personal distractions that may pop up and cause us to lose ourselves in the daily drama of life. **Hitting the Sweet Spot** isn't about ignoring these problems or distractions while you are at work—not at all! Instead, try to use your sense of awareness to strengthen your *inspiration* and *intention* under pressure: rather than becoming overwhelmed by potential chaos, rise to the challenge and see things through. The challenges you face today may change your tomorrow.

Now that you've taken some time to reflect on what you need to do to be aware of distractions and develop long-term *inspiration* at work, you may feel the impulse to ask yourself, "What can I do with the focus I'm feeling *right now*?!" Stick it out with me here, because the answer is nothing—yet.

Being aware of your potential distractions is one thing: knowing how to manage them is quite another.

Here are some practical methods for getting into the mindset for personal growth.

Shift your Thoughts

✓ Stop thinking about your distractions and shift your thoughts towards performing your work to your maximum potential.

✓ Tap into your sense of inspiration. Do a mental workout by giving yourself 10 minutes to engage in positive self-talk.

✓ Remember that every day is an opportunity to be amazing and have a "make it," not a "break it" attitude.

✓ Find a mantra that works for you and own it!

✓ Use the washroom as a resource. Look in the mirror, make eye contact, and believe it when you tell yourself that "you are amazing." Take a few moments to share a smile with the amazing person looking back at you.

✓ Take inventory of what you need to perform without distractions. When I was a host, my go-to kit included a pen, breath mints, and lip balm.

Create an Environment You Love

✓ Put photos of loved ones in your work area.

✓ If you can play music in the front or back of house, try to select an upbeat, welcoming soundtrack.

▪ If this isn't the case for your workplace, listen to the music that you love in your head. This can improve your mood significantly, especially if you're usually faced with silence or generic, service-friendly tunes.

✓ Do what you can to bring the sources of *your* joy into the workplace. This might include bringing a favourite book along for your lunch break and recommending it to others, baking cookies to share with your coworkers, or making conversation about the latest updates in your preferred sporting league. The key here is to share your joy and happiness, and to listen to the sources of your coworkers' joy, too!

Remember, "This Too Shall Pass"

✓ As Winston Churchill said, "if you're going through hell, keep going."

✓ Work on your ability to accept change, whether good or bad, as this will enable you to focus on your long-term intentions when things seem bleak.

✓ In a nutshell, nothing is ever as bad as it seems! Try to keep things in perspective by remembering to keep your focus on your intention.

Be Fun!

✓ Arrive at work with a smile and a sense of humour.

✓ Acknowledge that your workplace is a service environment, and that your attitude can have a significant impact on someone else's day.

✓ Laugh, laugh, laugh! Laughter is the best medicine.

▪ Don't divert your attentions from more important intentions and tasks by hiding behind having fun, however. Be up front and honest with yourself about your feelings and communicate to trustworthy friends, peers, or workplace superiors about your distractions when and if you can. In the meantime, though, there's nothing wrong with finding some shared pleasure in the joy of a joke and a communal feeling of happiness.

Articulating and proposing a new workplace process is done in steps. Typically, a strong recommendation is founded upon an understanding that the idea may enable the company to improve the current process, save money, provide awareness about health and safety regulations, and so on.

If you work with intention and focus, you will feel more confident that your job is something that you know inside and out. It's important to be conscious of your unique skills to fully appreciate what it is you have to offer at work. Now, you can add another tool to your belt by learning how to write a formal recommendation. By doing so, you can help your company improve, save money or increase profit, and provide skills and awareness to your coworkers. You will also strengthen your sense of intention by becoming involved with the brand's growth and long-term sustainability.

Offering recommendations often involves brainstorming about how to address needs and provide improvements to the current system. Try to see potential "problems" as a matter of perception: frame these distractions or bumps in the road as an opportunity to put your intention and inspiration to work.

Many executive decisions are made based on information gathered by experts in the fields of workplace efficiency, Human Resources, or related areas of study. In any hierarchically-structured company, someone in a position of authority will determine whether a recommendation will be accepted. While there are no guarantees that your recommendation will indeed improve the process, you won't know—or receive feedback—until you try.

✓ To improve productivity and increase profit for the organization.

✓ To increase associate employees' confidence in their work through further training or increased awareness of company regulations.

✓ To team-build, and to help others develop a sense of purpose at work.

✓ To show you care *for* your customers and are striving to work *with* your company.

✓ To show your gratitude for the opportunity to make the recommendation, and to continue to bring forth your ideas, because you never know—that one thought you share may be AMAZING!

Step 1: State and Seize the Opportunity

Provide a detailed account of the current system. Describe the environment and the process at hand without bias—remember that there are never problems, only opportunities. The current system is in place for a reason; it may be the case that there has never been a recommendation to offer something different, so beware of the precedent for pursuing this action in your workplace.

Step 2: Introduce Your Recommendation

Give a detailed account of the recommendation, including the cost, time, and labour required, if any. Be aware of the risk of unknown-unknowns. Being in a frontline position, there are many details that may be tied up in the process you want to improve which you may not know about, including other departments' policies and procedures. Knowledge of your position will guide you in formulating a recommendation. Request feedback from your superior for clarification as to why your recommendation may or may not be implemented, without any emotional attachment to the outcome.

Step 3: Describe the Implications of the Recommendation

Take the time to articulate how your recommendation will accomplish the goals outlined in the "Why Offer a Recommendation?" section. Emphasize the value of your idea while maintaining a respectful, open-minded tone.

Putting the Pieces Together

Focus that is driven by a sense of genuine inspiration is what is needed to make a meaningful recommendation. When you feel obligated to work, and you lack motivation, it's hard to find the passion needed to put your ideas forth and turn your intention into action. Put simply, it's about trying to see things through rose-tinted glasses, not green ones: hearts, not dollars, will help you "plant for eternity," not just tomorrow.

It's tempting to see businesses as faceless, monolithic, and disinterested in their individual employees. If you think that way, though, you tend to manifest your own worst nightmares in the workplace. If you consider yourself to be more than a number, and act accordingly, you can **Hit the Sweet Spot** every time you clock in. You are valuable. Your ideas matter. If you work with inspiration and intention, you can get the job done.

When your attitude is right, you care about your work, and you are ready to focus, you will be fully prepared to take responsibility for yourself—and others— in times both good and not-so-good.

Chapter 4

Responsibility

"Working with love and loving your work are two different things. When you work with love you work with gratitude."

—*Evelyn Waterhouse*

TAKING RESPONSIBILITY FOR YOUR actions and reactions is one of the most humbling things you can do in your personal and professional relationships. Understanding the difference between fault and responsibility is crucial when trying to **Hit the Sweet Spot.** Waiting for someone else to take initiative or assume blame for a situation is a motivation deflator. It is up to you to start developing a habitual mindset that allows you to recognize that you are responsible for your actions and their impact (even when this impact was unintentional), especially when working with others. Responsibility is the final ingredient in our recipe, and, of all four of the necessary components for **Hitting the Sweet Spot**, it is perhaps the most difficult to add to the bubbling pot.

How does taking responsibility help you as a frontline professional? When you take responsibility for yourself, you are taking charge of writing the history of who you are as a person. When I realized this, I embraced a go-to set of reminders that I like to call the *Four P's*, which have never failed to keep me at the top of my game and ready to take responsibility for myself: Presentable, Prepared, Punctual, and Present. The *Four P's* are paramount in encouraging your customers and your superiors to trust in you as a workplace professional and as a person. Keeping them in mind while you are preparing for work and going about your tasks during the day will strengthen your ability to take responsibility for your actions and inspire others to trust in your sense of self and integrity.

Presentable

Take the time to ensure that your personal hygiene is better than just "up to snuff." Make sure you've showered: wash your hair, apply a little left and right guard, and keep a clean uniform ready. Present yourself in the best possible way: every day is your responsibility, and an opportunity to make others see you the way you want to be seen. This *P* will make you feel good about yourself while also demonstrating respect for your company's brand, your co-workers, and your customers.

Prepared

What tools do you need to have on your person while at work to ensure that you have a productive shift? Some go-to items while I worked in Hospitality included pens, order pads, documents related to shift handovers, and so on. It's also important to stay in the loop with workplace developments, promotions, and upcoming events. Taking the time to get caught up with the company and its happenings shows that you care about how you represent you.

Punctual

People's time is important—and so is yours! Know when your shifts start and do whatever you have to do to be on time. Nothing is more challenging and frustrating for your team, be it your supervisor or co-workers, than staff not arriving for their shifts in a punctual manner. Show responsibility by being on time not only when you arrive at work, but also when you leave for and return from your breaks. Remember to be mindful: don't take advantage of a co-worker's offer to "cover" for you just for an extra five minutes of rest. There's plenty of time for that when you clock out.

Present

Be present while you are at work. Just like in Focus, where we discussed developing a sense of intention that can transcend distractions, bring this inspiration with you every time you enter the workplace. Everyone has a life outside of work and personal developments can be challenging to let go of, or to not dwell upon. Understand who you are and who you are not: if these external events are impacting you significantly, seek help from a trusted friend, loved one, or counsellor. Being responsible means taking care of what is happening outside of your workplace; it is the greatest gift you can give yourself. Not everything is doom and gloom, of course, but having a positive and present frame of mind going into work will set the stage for the rest of your time there. Being present it is the gift that keeps on giving—even if it means taking the steps for long-term change at work by addressing the personal distractions in your life.

"*Oh baby, why don't you just meet me in the middle?*

I'm losing my mind just a little

So, why don't you meet me in the middle?"

—*Zedd*

B E RESPONSIBLE FOR YOU. DON'T MAKE any excuses. Don't wait for others to take the blame for your actions, and don't hesitate to accept fault for accidents in which you were complicit or directly involved. Never be disingenuous when taking responsibility for yourself or your team. Working in the Hospitality Industry and developing the skills to know how and when to compromise is what it means to **Hit the Sweet Spot**. Working *with* people is about understanding that, for frontline associates, it is important to have a "meet me in the middle" attitude towards superiors; it is not about "US" versus "THEM," but rather what "WE" can do together to create amazing customer experiences. Let's meet in the middle, from the top down and the bottom up.

What's at stake when you take Responsibility for yourself? Let's break it down.

Your Reputation

How do you want to be seen as a coworker or frontline associate? Do you want others to recognize you as a hard worker, and as someone that gets the job done? Would you prefer to be known for working smart and being a strong team player? You can make this happen— when you put in the effort, be patient, and understand that taking responsibility for yourself is a major step along the way to achieving these goals.

Your Job

This is YOUR job! Are you preforming your duties to the best of your abilities? Are you fulfilling the description of your job outlined for you by your employer? Are you communicating your needs to the company in order to ensure better results in the long run? **Hitting the Sweet Spot** is about so much more than clocking in, completing the bare minimum, and collecting a pay cheque for your "effort." You can make positive changes happen when you take initiative, believe in yourself, and bring new ideas to the attention of your superiors.

Your Company

Believe it or not, you made the choice to work at your place of employment at some point or another! Whether the reasons for doing so included the pay, location, hours, or benefits, when you took on this position you chose to be responsible for upholding the company's expectations of their brand and employees. If you find that you do not personally mesh with the culture of your workplace—or with frontline service as a whole—you have the choice to work elsewhere. If you are not happy where you work that negativity will spread throughout the company.

Your Life

This is your life, and how you choose to live it is your choice. Take responsibility for where you work, what you do, and how you do it—for yourself, and for the people around you. Develop a strong sense of self-control and be mindful of the ways in which you can control your attitude and actions. When we take control, we refuse to be victims of circumstance, or of our own personal weaknesses. Self-control and self-discipline will also keep you from making excuses for yourself. We can take charge of our lives and of the situations that we face. This is a principal requirement for writing your own story and **Hitting the Sweet Spot** on your own terms.

No Excuses

Simply put, there is no good excuse for having a bad attitude at work. I'm not going to repeat Chapter 1, but I will say this: if you're walking into your workplace with an attitude that is negative, then really take some time to reflect on why and how you've come to feel that way. Put these feelings in a box inside your head somewhere and take a step back before you try to figure this out.

I'm going to share a story with you regarding attitude, and perpetuating what it is that you dislike about the organization in which you work instead of inspiring positive change. I had been working with a gentleman who was recently promoted to a supervisory role and one day he was just going on and on:

"This place is horrible! I can't stand it. I hate it. I'm sick of and tired of listening to complaints, and I'm sick and tired of listening to people. All they do all day long is complain, complain, and complain. It's just horrendous."

Listening to his angry venting, I realized that his attitude about his job was undoubtedly perpetuating exactly what he disliked in others. It's hard to take it seriously when someone complains about other peoples' complaints!

There's a phrase I love that fits perfectly here: *there's something about you that I don't like about me.* If you really think about that for a second, what my coworker disliked in his position was now being forced upon others. When I realized this, I approached him.

"I'm going to ask you a question," I said. "I'm going to say the same thing to you that I would say to anybody in any position acting the way you're acting. If you don't like where you are, then get out. If it's too hot in the kitchen, leave."

It was important to me to make him recognize that, by complaining in this way, he was making his coworkers deal with exactly what caused him so much frustration. My coworker was grateful for my input and eventually changed his outlook. This lesson is especially important when you're working in front of people: you may think anything you like about your coworkers on your own time, but it really is so much better to truly feel that you're grateful, and that you are taking on your role with intention. Sometimes you need to change your attitude about your work and learn to adapt in order to embrace it. Be willing to make miss-takes and learn along the way. These are integral steps towards taking responsibility for yourself and **Hitting the Sweet Spot**.

Can you truly look at someone else and feel joyful for them and their success without impeding your own? Or do you look at other people and say, "Why are they getting promoted?"; "Why are they getting that job?"; "Why do they get to do that?" It's hard to trust in your own capabilities and celebrate others without becoming envious. Just like the four chapters in this book, though, it's important to remember that every individual is important and has something to offer, and that we all need to come together to **Hit the Sweet Spot**. Everyone has gifts and skills that make them unique.

Of course, it'd be nice for everyone to be treated equally regardless of what they bring to the table at work, but the reality of it is, we're just not the same. Some people know their *thing* inside and out and are at the top of their field because of the work and time they've devoted to their practice. Remember the master chef? It's a real balancing act of humility and kindness to recognize the strengths of others while also learning to see your own shortcomings or the skills you'd like to improve upon. So, how do we do this? How do we recognize in ourselves what we can see and celebrate freely in others?

Start by reflecting on your own values. What traits do you admire in yourself and others? By getting in touch with the characteristics you appreciate in others, you can more clearly see what it is about yourself that you'd like to improve. Rather than becoming docile and passive or uptight and aggressive, use self-control and self-reflection to control your behaviour and aspire to hold yourself higher and more meaningfully.

Aggression can only get you so far. A lot of people will say that aggression in the workplace is a good thing: it shows that you're dedicated, and that you want movement. But this isn't the case in every company, and the "dog eat dog" mentality depends entirely on the culture of your company. I personally prefer working with companies that have more of an environment of consensus between managerial and frontline staff, and in which we can use creativity. I came to this realization when I reflected on my preferences and needs in the workplace and took responsibility for ensuring that my values were represented in my company. We are all capable of self-control, and we can all use it to articulate our needs without causing the pendulum to swing from one emotional extreme to the other. Knowing yourself and internalizing your values can help you reach a new level of self-awareness and become more aware that you have something unique and amazing to offer to your company.

Recognizing what you have to offer also means treating yourself with self-respect. This involves knowing when to speak up for yourself if your needs aren't being meet in the workplace. The qualities that a strong friendly and personable frontline associate possess are similar to the qualities that people seek in personal relationships.

Because of this, though, it can become challenging to navigating workplace friendships and flirtations.

Self-Control

I want to share a story with you regarding a former customer that I used to truly enjoy seating. Our interactions were always cheerful and genuine, but one day he made a comment accompanied by a wink and a smile that rubbed me the wrong way: "Boy, you're trouble, aren't you?"

With that wink and a smile, I knew that I had a choice to make. There's no taking back what's been said—you can only move forward. I had to decide how to handle this customer without drawing too much attention to the situation, and with an entirely different perspective on our relationship. In the end, I chose to graciously smile. I told him, "I'd prefer to be called sunshine, because I am not trouble for you or anybody else here. I'm sunshine and that's what I prefer to be called."

That experience established a precedent for this external customer. He learned that I take responsibility for myself and how I would like to be treated. In that moment, I took ownership of how I would be perceived, and how I wanted others to treat me. It took self-control to not react with indignation, and at the same time to not undermine my own reputation by letting it go or just laughing it off. It is a skill for every man and woman to be responsible for creating balance. Be assertive without aggression. Be humble without losing your dignity and laughing everything off, or saying it doesn't matter, because it does. Now, there may be times when an exchange like this one could be taken a step too far: if it gets to that point, you may want to bring the situation to the attention of your supervisor. If you have done what you can to address the issue, explain this, and relay that you have tried to bring awareness to your customer—or coworker—that their behaviour is inappropriate.

Every workplace is unique, and how these issues are handled is a huge testament to the culture of the company, especially during the current #MeToo Movement. It is no longer acceptable to ignore sexism or harassment in the workplace: if your company won't take responsibility for its own policies and procedures, seriously reevaluate your choice to remain its employee. Of course, we as frontline associates want to be mindful of how we go about bringing these situations to light to our supervisors. Remember to be assertive, not passive or aggressive. You don't want to be perceived as someone who complains every other day, so take responsibility for yourself when you can: often, with good communication skills and self-control, you will be able handle these things on your own.

You can take also personal responsibility at work in a different, more definite way: by accepting that the situation at hand just isn't ideal for you. Whether this means the job itself or a process that's been implemented, you can make the choice to speak up for yourself. You don't have to stay! You can always find someplace else to work, but if you have a company or organization that values and respects you and has typically taken steps to accommodate your needs, be grateful and try not to throw it away too quickly. When you do feel this way, taking responsibility for something you may disagree with about the company can pose a unique personal challenge. It's important to look at the big picture in these situations. For me, looking at the big picture means thinking in terms of the customer. It also means thinking about long-term company sustainability. What can I do to make this organization be around for generations to come—and how can I make sure that they, too, are **Hitting the Sweet Spot** as the years go by?

It can be challenging to inspire others to think this way. How can we create major shifts in employees' attitudes, and encourage our coworkers to take on the responsibility to do so? In my experience as a mother of four, I've learned the importance of thinking about your family beyond the "now." In the same way, you should think of your company as you want it to function in the future. It's difficult to think this way if you're operating on a mindset of merely clocking in, doing your job, and heading home for the day. It's so important to bring the four ingredients of **Hitting the Sweet Spot** together to work through the temptation to simply come to and leave work without thinking of the impact on coworkers and customers that you could make along the way.

I work *for* the person who signs my pay cheque, and I work *with* everybody else: customers, fellow frontline staff, supervisors, management, and so on. When I come to work, I check my attitude. I ask whether I am prepared to care for and focus on my job. With this awareness, I can take full responsibility for my actions.

Encouraging everyone to be on the same page is a challenge, but who doesn't love a challenge?

With this book, we'll face it together.

Thank you.